40 Prayers For Athletes

40 PRAYERS TO GLORIFY THE LORD AND STEWARD YOUR ATHLETIC ABILITY FOR THE KINGDOM

WRITTEN BY JAE TAFT

WWW.COACHJAETAFT.COM

Introduction

IF THERE WAS ONE THING I WOULD GO BACK AND REDO
DURING MY TIME BEING AN ATHLETE IT WOULD BE KEEPING
GOD AT THE CENTER. UNDERSTANDING THAT HE IS THE
SOURCE AND WORTHY OF PRAISE THROUGH ALL THINGS.
NOT JUST A VICTORY ON THE COURT OR A GREAT GAME
BUT THROUGH THE HEARTACHE OF SPORTS, AND THE HURT
FROM TEAMMATES AND COACHES. AND THE DOUBT THAT
SOMETIMES BECOMES VERY REAL.

I BELIEVE THAT GOD DESERVES AND IS WORTHY OF OUR
PRAISE. I AM ALSO FEELING VERY HEAVY ON MY HEART THAT
GOD IS BEING TREATED MORE AS A GENIE THAN OUR LORD
IN THE ATHLETIC WORLD. I AM CALLING ON YOU, MY
FELLOW CHRISTIAN ATHLETES, TO LIFT THE NAME OF JESUS
IN EVERYTHING WE DO.

WE KNOW OUR WEAPON IS PRAYER. THAT IS WHY I CREATED
THIS 40-DAY PRAYER JOURNAL. TO UNCOVER THE POWER OF
PRAYER AND ENCOURAGE YOU TO GET IN CONVERSATION
WITH GOD. HE CARES ABOUT WHAT'S ON YOUR HEART, THE
THINGS YOU GO THROUGH, AND THE THOUGHTS YOU HAVE
TROUBLE PUTTING INTO WORDS.

YOUR DESIRE TO FIND THE RIGHT SCHOOL TO PLAY
COLLEGE SPORTS AT, THE COACH THAT HURT YOU, OR THE
DOUBT IN YOUR ATHLETIC ABILITY ARE ALL THINGS GOD
CARES TO TAKE THE BURDEN FOR.

I CAN'T WAIT FOR YOU TO GO THROUGH THESE NEXT 40
DAYS AND DIVE INTO DEEP, RAW, AND AUTHENTIC
CONVERSATION WITH THE LORD. IT'S ABOUT TO BE
AMAZING AND I AM SO EXCITED FOR YOU!

Glorifying The Lord While Playing

[1 CORINTHIANS 10:31]

So whether you eat or drink or whatever
you do, do it all for the glory of God.

Dear Lord,

I first off want to thank You for the opportunity and ability to play the sport I love. I know I can take for granted the opportunity to play and I ask for forgiveness for that. God I want to glorify You through my athletic ability whether that is in a game, practice, a conversation with a teammate, or a training session. I pray that You help remind me that I can vessel for your kingdom while using my athletic ability at the same time. God, I pray you open opportunities for me to put on display Your goodness and love to those who may not know You. I want to glorify Your name through all that I do and that includes my athletic ability. In Your name, I pray, Amen!

Glorifying The Lord While Playing

Staying Disciplined

[HEBREWS 12:11]

For the moment all discipline seems
painful rather than pleasant, but later it
yields the peaceful fruit of righteousness
to those who have been trained by it.

Staying Disciplined

Dear Lord,

I pray over my discipline as an athlete. I pray Hebrews 12:11 over my life. Even though discipline can be a hard practice to lean into I know that there will be peace in the harvest of those who are trained in this way. God in the way that I strive to display discipline in my athletic career, I even more so want it in my relationship with You. Lord, I need Your strength to help me stay disciplined in my training. Whether that is dedicating time to Your word every day, pushing through the last rep even when I want to give up, making sure I am getting enough sleep, or filling my body with the best foods I can. I want to reap the harvest You have for me, Lord. I pray that the practice of living a disciplined life only leads to glorifying Your name. Amen!

Staying Disciplined

Loving Teammates & Coaches Well

[JOHN 13:34]

A new command I give you: Love one
another. As I have loved you, so you must
love one another.

Loving Teammates & Coaches Well

Dear Lord,

I pray that Your love is on display by how I love my coaches and teammates. Guide me in Your love. I know that there can be times when I am frustrated with my coach or teammate but God I want to love them well. I need your strength God to be slow to anger but quick in love. And if there's a tough conversion that needs to be had, I pray that it's covered in love and not words of death. God, I also want to ask for forgiveness when I haven't been a loving teammate and I strive to be better. Thank You for the opportunity to have a team that I can go on the court every game and compete with. Thank You for your endless love for me and I pray my teammates and coaches feel Your love through me. I love You, Lord. Amen!

Loving Teammates & Coaches Well

Serving My Teammates & Coaches Well

[ROMANS 12:10]

Be devoted to one another in love. Honor
one another above yourselves.

Serving My Teammates & Coaches Well

Dear God,

I am inspired by and want to serve my teammates and coaches like Matthew 25:35-40 states. Athletics can turn quickly into a self-idolizing and all-about-me type of journey. And God I first pray and ask for forgiveness if I have headed down that route and I ask for your guidance out of that. Playing sports is an incredible way to serve others and bring glory to Your kingdom. Lord, I pray that I not only be the first person to jump on an opportunity to serve my team but that I seek it out. Whether that is to fill a water bottle up for a teammate, clean the gym of trash after the game, rebound for a teammate getting extra shots, or help my coach put the basketball away. God help remind me that playing sports is much more than any achievement I gain. It's about serving my team with the love You have put on the example for me. Thank You, God. Amen!

Serving My Teammates & Coaches Well

Gratitude For The Body I Was Gifted

[PSALM 139:13-14]

For you formed my inward parts; you knitted me together in my mother's womb. I praise you, for I am fearfully and wonderfully made. Wonderful are your works; my soul knows it very well.

Gratitude For The Body I Was Gifted

Dear God,

Thank You for the body that I have. A body that is a gift given by your grace. A body that can run, jump, and get in a defensive stance. Lord thank you for declaring my body good. It is good because you have created it. I pray that I am glorifying you God through my body and how I treat it. And I know that I can mistreat it. Whether that is fueling my body right, resting my body, or speaking life-giving words over my body God I want to glorify You with this temple You have given me. Thank you for creating me in my mother's womb and giving me the athletic ability to play the sport I love so much. I love You, God. Amen!

Gratitude For The Body I Was Gifted

_____

_____

_____

_____

_____

_____

_____

_____

_____

_____

_____

_____

_____

_____

_____

_____

_____

_____

_____

_____

_____

_____

_____

_____

_____

_____

Being A Light On The Court

You, LORD, keep my lamp burning; my God turns my darkness into light.

Dear Lord,

I want to be a light for your kingdom. I pray that you fill me Holy Spirit. As I step onto the court for practice or games I pray that you shine through me. I pray that opponents leave playing against me feeling something different. If there is an opportunity to talk about You to others I pray you open that door. Flow to me so you can flow through me, God. I pray that it's Your words that are spoken and not mine. Lord I love your kingdom and I am open for You to use me as a vessel whenever and wherever you need me. I love you, God. Amen!

Being A Light On The Court

Stewarding My Athletic Ability Well

[EPHESIANS 2:10]

For we are God's handiwork, created in Christ Jesus to do good works, which God prepared in advance for us to do.

Dear God,

Thank You for the opportunity to play the sport I love. I pray that I never take it for granted and if I do please convict me on the spot. I want to steward my athletic ability well because I know it's a way that I can glorify You. It's so cool that I can glorify You through athletics. God show me new ways to continue to steward this gift. Whether that's being more disciplined in my training, resting well, or serving my teammates better. It's all about bringing glory to You and Your kingdom. Please guide my heart to be in the right posture where it's aligned with your kingdom's mission. I love you, God, Amen!

To Steward My Athletic Ability Well

Finishing The Race

[ROMANS 5:3-4]

Not only that, but we rejoice in our sufferings, knowing that suffering produces endurance, and endurance produces character, and character produces hope,

Finishing The Race

Dear Lord,

I pray for the strength to finish a workout or a game well. I know there are times when I catch myself watching the clock until practice ends or wanting to quit a drill early. God I pray for the strength to push past the want to quit. Help me finish the race well. Both athletically and spiritually. Please forgive me for the times that I have not stewarded my practice time well. God, You have given me a gift to use my body to perform athletically and I want to glorify You in that gift. I also ask the Lord that You help me recognize when a teammate needs encouragement at a time when they are doubting if they can finish the workout well. Thank You, God, for your endless amount of encouragement over my life. I love You, Lord. Amen!

Finishing The Race

_____
_____
_____
_____
_____
_____
_____
_____
_____
_____
_____
_____
_____
_____
_____
_____
_____
_____
_____
_____
_____
_____
_____

Praying Against Pre-Game Anxiety

[1 PETER 5:6-7]

Humble yourselves, therefore, under the mighty hand of God so that at the proper time he may exalt you, casting all your anxieties on him, because he cares for you.

Praying Against Pre-Game Anxiety

Dear Lord,

I pray in Your precious name Jesus that any anxiety flees from my mind before my game. Fear does not run my life, but Your truth does. I know anxious thoughts are not from You God. We know from Your words that power is in the tongue. I pray that in times of anxiousness, Your words of truth flood my mind. I am capable, I am equipt, I am a child of the king most high. Help me remember that as much as I want to perform well in my game Your love for me does not waiver. I could play the best game or the worst game and I still know that You love me just the same. Remind me Lord of all the preparation I have put into my skills to go out and play well. I am prepared. Help me play free and fearless God. I love You, Lord. Amen.

Praying Against Pre-Game Anxiety

_____

_____

_____

_____

_____

_____

_____

_____

_____

_____

_____

_____

_____

_____

_____

_____

_____

_____

_____

_____

_____

_____

_____

_____

Identity Found In Christ

[1 PETER 2:9]

But you are a chosen race, a royal priesthood, a holy nation, a people for his own possession, that you may proclaim the excellencies of him who called you out of darkness into his marvelous light.

Identity Found In Christ

Dear God,

Thank You for knitting me in my mother's womb. For I know I was made by the Creator of the universe and You have called me Yours. God, it can be hard to not wrap my identity in who I am as an athlete. But I ask that You please help me remember that I am Your child first. Remind me to never place my identity in a sport that can be taken away from me and will end one day. But knowing the truth that my identity as Your child can never be taken away. It is a gift You have freely given me. I am Your child. I am chosen. I am called. I am set apart. Thank You, God, for the opportunity to play the sport I love. I praise You over and over again! I love You, Lord. Amen!

Identity Found In Christ

Thankfulness To Compete

[1 THESSALONIANS 5:18]

Give thanks in all circumstances; for this is the will
of God in Christ Jesus for you.

Thankfulness To Compete

Dear God,

I simply just want to thank You. I want to spend a moment in gratitude for the opportunity to play and compete in the sport I love. Thank You for a healthy body, the people around me who believe in me, and the athletic ability You have gifted me. God, I pray that my heart is postured to glorify You through my athletics and to never take this for granted. Whether that is in a game, practice, or conversation with the opponent I pray that I shine Your light. Thank you, God, for the ability to express myself athletically. What a special time in my life. I love You, Lord. Amen!

Thankfulness To Compete

Life-giving Thoughts

[COLOSSIANS 3:2-5]

Set your minds on things above, not on earthly things.

Life-giving Thoughts

Dear God,

Thank You for the reminder that there is power in the words we speak and think to ourselves. I need the reminder of grace over my life. I can be so hard on myself. God, I need help being reminded that there is room for grace in my life. I pray out the negative thoughts in Jesus' name. And that Your words of life and truth would flush the bad ones out. You are life, the living water, the one that refreshes my soul. Anything in my life that is not from You I pray it goes away. I am not a failure because I missed a free throw. I am Your child and You created me for so much more. I love You, God, Amen!

Life-giving Thoughts

_____

_____

_____

_____

_____

_____

_____

_____

_____

_____

_____

_____

_____

_____

_____

_____

_____

_____

_____

_____

_____

_____

My Worth Is In Jesus, Not My Stats

[PSALM 139:14]

I praise you because I am fearfully and wonderfully made; your works are wonderful, I know that full well

Dear Lord,

Remind me of the truth regarding my worth. My worth is not in my performance, not in the number of points I score, not in how my coaches see me. My worth is found in You. In that, I was created by and for the Creator. God thank you for seeing me as precious no matter what my performance looks like on the court. God, You are the ultimate scorekeeper and I know I am loved, chosen, and seen by You. Let Your truth about who I am be known higher than anything the world says about me. I love You and praise You, Lord. Amen!

My Worth Is In Jesus, Not My Stats

_____
_____
_____
_____
_____
_____
_____
_____
_____
_____
_____
_____
_____
_____
_____
_____
_____
_____
_____
_____
_____
_____
_____
_____
_____
_____
_____

Safety Traveling To Games

[LUKE 4:10]

Scripture says, 'He will put his angels in charge of you to watch over you carefully.

Safety Traveling To Games

Dear Lord,

I pray for the safety of my team, the opponent, the refs, and the fans as we travel to our games. I pray covering our buses and cars and we drive there. I know sometimes the weather conditions aren't ideal but we can't control that. I pray over the bus drivers as they sacrifice their time to bring our team to the games. Please keep them alert of the road ahead and covered in your safety. Thank You God for Your covering. I love You, Lord. Amen

Safety Traveling To Games

Grace In My Athletic Journey

[2 PETER 1:2]

Grace and peace be yours in abundance through the knowledge of God and of Jesus our Lord.

Grace In My Athletic Journey

Dear Lord,

I need Your help with grace. God, I know that
You have so much grace for me when I don't
deserve it. Your grace and mercy over my life is
such a sweet gift. I mess up all the time and You
remind me that there are new mercies each
morning. Help me in the area of my athletic
journey where grace is hard for me to accept.
Help me be reminded that missing a shot,
having a bad practice, or messing up a play is
part of the journey and will happen. I hold
myself to be perfect when I know only Jesus is.
Remind me that grace is a key part of the
process and is needed in my life. I love You,
Lord. Amen!

Grace In My Athletic Journey

Patience In My Skill Development

[COLOSSIANS 1:10-11]

We're praying this so that you can live lives that are worthy of the Lord and pleasing to him in every way: by producing fruit in every good work and growing in the knowledge of God; by being strengthened through his glorious might so that you endure everything and have patience.

Patience In My Skill Development

Dear God,

I need Your patience over my life. There are parts in my development journey as an athlete that are so hard. I get frustrated when I am not nailing a skill and I tend to speak poorly of myself. God give me the strength to patiently endure this season of life where my skills are being refined and molded. Just like my walk with You. Help me resist laziness and instead work hard at the task ahead, such as building my skillset. I pray that I am reminded of how this is an opportunity to lean on You and steward this athletic ability well for the Kingdom, I need You. I love you, Lord. Amen.

Patience In My Skill Development

Praying Over Injuries

[ISAIAH 40:29]

He gives strength to the weary
and increases the power of the weak.

Praying Over Injuries

Dear God,

I want to take a moment to pray over injuries. Whether that is for myself or my teammates God I pray healing over their bodies. I pray for a recovery that leads to an even stronger comeback to the injured body part. I also pray that during this time off from playing You cover myself or my teammates in peace and comfort reminding us that we still have value even if we aren't getting minutes on the floor. We know God that You can teach and refine us so much during this time. Reveal to those who have an injury how important rest is. How this is a moment where we can spend distraction-free with You. I pray for healing over the injury. I love You, God. Amen!

Praying Over Injuries

God's Will For Me To Play In College

[PROVERBS 3:5-6]

Trust in the LORD with all your heart and lean not on your own understanding; in all your ways submit to him, and he will make your paths straight.

God's Will For Me To Play In College

Dear Lord,

I want to submit to You my goal of playing college athletics. I know how easy it can be to let goals of mine become an idol in my life and that's not what I want. God, I pray that if it is Your will for me to play in college You open the door. Place my name in the coach's office of the college I am supposed to play for. I pray for a coach who cares about me as a human and my development as an athlete. I pray for a team that is an extension of my family. And I pray that I am shown the right school You need me to be at, Lord. I thank You for the opportunity to play the sport I love. I love You, Lord. Amen!

God's Will For Me To Play In College

_____

_____

_____

_____

_____

_____

_____

_____

_____

_____

_____

_____

_____

_____

_____

_____

_____

_____

_____

_____

_____

_____

_____

_____

Prayer For The Coach Who Hurt You

[MATTHEW 6:14-15]

For if you forgive others their trespasses, your heavenly Father will also forgive you, but if you do not forgive others their trespasses, neither will your Father forgive your trespasses.

Prayer For The Coach Who Hurt You

Dear God,

I need Your strength for true forgiveness. I know that I can only find this in You. It's really hard for my flesh to want to forgive this coach that hurt me. But I know Jesus gave His life for me, so I am called to forgive as a follower of You. God remove the hate in my heart and replace it with love. For we know that love covers a multitude of sins and there is power in Your Love. God, I want to walk like Jesus did, and I know this requires forgiveness. Thank You for Your daily forgiveness of my sins and for sending Your precious son on the cross. To forgive us once and for all. I love You, Lord. Amen!

Prayer For The Coach Who Hurt You

Forgiveness To A Teammate Who Hurt Me

[EPHESIANS 4:32]

Be kind to one another, tenderhearted, forgiving one another, as God in Christ forgave you.

Forgiveness To A Teammate Who Hurt Me

Dear God,

I need Your strength to forgive my teammate who hurt me. God, it's not the situation I want to be in and my flesh wants to seek justice myself. But God I know You are the ultimate ruler of justice and You fight my battles. I pray to deny my flesh in moments where forgiveness is very hard. Help me lead with love just as You do for me when I break your heart. God, I need You at this moment to help mold my heart to be one that leads with forgiveness and doesn't harbor bitterness. Thank You, Lord, for Your forgiveness over my life. I love You, Amen!

Forgivness To A Teammate Who Hurt Me

Fight Against Fear

[2 TIMOTHY 1:7]

For God gave us a spirit not of fear but of power
and love and self-control.

Dear God,

I pray over the fight against fear in my mind. Whether that is fear before a game, fear to make a mistake, or fear that I am not good enough. God, Your word clearly states that fear is not from You. So if I lead with fear in how I play the game, I am not leading with Your truth. I am leaning into the lies of the enemy at that point and that's not okay. God, I pray that every day I wake up I put on Your armor and fight. Whether that's the battle on the court or a spiritual battle. Knowing that I am fighting for victory and not for it. Help me play free and with joy. Fill me with Your joy, God. I love You, Amen!

Fight Against Fear

Strength When I Want To Give Up

[2 CORINTHIANS 12:9]

My grace is all you need, for my power is the greatest when you are weak.

Strength When I Want To Give Up

Dear God,

Help me fight the want to give up. When the enemy tries to plant lies that I am not good enough, I can't finish this rep, or I should just quit the sport I love, I pray that your truth comes flooding into my life. I pray God that You place people in my life who call me higher and pray over those thoughts that aren't from You. I pray God that it is Your peace that directs my timeline for being an athlete. And that I will obey when You call me to move on to the next season of my life. In Jesus' name, I pray that it is Your peace that guides me in my athletic career and timeline. I need only Your strength to push through the hard moments. I love You, Lord. Amen!

Strength When I Want To Give Up

_____

_____

_____

_____

_____

_____

_____

_____

_____

_____

_____

_____

_____

_____

_____

_____

_____

_____

_____

_____

_____

_____

Slow To Anger

[JAMES 1:19-20]

My dear brothers and sisters, take note of this:
Everyone should be quick to listen, slow to speak and
slow to become angry, because human anger does not
produce the righteousness that God desires.

Dear Lord,

You call us to be slow to anger and slow to speak. There are times when I forget that. In the heat of the moment, I am quick to be angry and I speak poorly to my teammates. God, first I ask for forgiveness for letting my anger get the best of me. But second I ask for the strength to not speak my mind right off the bat. I also ask for the patience to choose my words wisely. Help me lead with loving comments to my teammates. Help me encourage them instead of blaming my teammates. Help me lower my pride and call my teammates higher. Lead me to have a heart that is full of life-giving words instead of life-sucking comments. I love You, Lord. Amen

Slow To Anger

Slow To Anger Towards The Refs + My Opponents

[PROVERBS 14:17]

People with a hot temper do foolish things; wiser people remain calm.

Slow To Anger Towards The Refs + My Opponents

Dear Lord,

There are many moments where I act out of frustration, pride, and anger which leads me to act not the best towards a ref or an opponent. God help me find the balance of being competitive, standing up for myself, and being a light for the kingdom. Help me to remember that refs are people who make mistakes just like I do. Even if I don't agree with their call, help me have a heart posture that resembles how Jesus would act. I pray that I lead with humility instead of pride in all things. I love You, Lord. Amen!

Slow To Anger Towards The Refs + My Opponents

_____

_____

_____

_____

_____

_____

_____

_____

_____

_____

_____

_____

_____

_____

_____

_____

_____

_____

_____

_____

_____

_____

_____

Athletics Being An Idol

[JONAH 2:8]

Those who cling to worthless idols turn away from God's love for them.

Athletics Being An Idol

Dear Lord,

Please forgive me for all the times I put my sport over You. Whether that is finding my identity in who I am as an athlete, equaling my worth to what's on the stat sheet, or believing I am better than anyone because of my athletic performance. I never want to place my identity in something that can be taken away from me. God, I know that you are the only thing that cannot be taken away from me. I pray and ask that You guide my heart to knowing that You are the Lord over my life. Not my sport or any accomplishment I have done. Thank You for Your unwavering love for me. I love you, Lord, Amen!

Athletics Being An Idol

Fighting The Fear Of Failure

[ISAIAH 41:10]

Fear not, for I am with you; be not dismayed, for I am your God; I will strengthen you, I will help you, I will uphold you with my righteous right hand.

Fighting The Fear Of Failure

Dear Lord,

I need You in the fight of the fear of failure that I have. Remind me that no game whether I play good or bad determines my eternal life with you in Heaven. Because of this reminder, I can't truly fail on the court. Lord help me to remember that I have to make mistakes to learn truly how to be a better athlete. Help me rewrite what failure is and isn't in your eyes. Lead me with a thought pattern that wants to learn and grow and understand what the developmental process takes to reach the next level in my athletic career. God, I thank You for Your truth over my life and Your endless love You give me. I love you, Lord. Amen.

Fighting The Fear Of Failure

_____
_____
_____
_____
_____
_____
_____
_____
_____
_____
_____
_____
_____
_____
_____
_____
_____
_____
_____
_____
_____
_____
_____

Focus During The Game

Let your eyes look straight ahead; fix your
gaze directly before you.

Dear God,

I pray for a still mind during my game. I pray that any negative thought or distraction will flee in Jesus' name. Help me stay focused on the task ahead and lead me in thoughts that are from You. When my mind starts to wonder I pray that you bring it back to the present moment. Knowing that all I have is the present time and to steward it well. I love you, Lord. Amen!

Focus During The Game

Prayer For Your Coach's Leadership

[HEBREWS 13:17]

Trust in your leaders. Put yourselves under their authority. Do this, because they keep watch over you. They know they are accountable to God for everything they do. Do this, so that their work will be a joy. If you make their work a heavy load, it won't do you any good.

Prayer For Your Coach's Leadership

Dear God,

I pray over my coach and their leadership. I pray that they lead our team well with love, discipline, and courage. I pray over the silent battles they may face that I have no clue of. I pray over any insecurities they may be facing while trying to lead our team. I pray for encouragement over their life knowing that coaching isn't the easiest job. I pray for life-giving words to speak to my coach. I pray for patience with my coach knowing that they might need it during challenging times over the course of our season. God, please convict me if I let my pride get in the way of their leadership. Reminding myself that they are a person in need of Your grace and love. I love You, God. Amen!

Prayer For Your Coach's Leadership

Encouraging Words For My Team

[1 THESSALONIANS 5:11]

Therefore encourage one another and build
each other up, just as in fact you are doing.

Dear God,

I pray that You fill my heart with the right words of encouragement to speak over my team. That words of the wicked are like a murderous ambush, but words of the godly save lives (Proverbs 12:6). I pray for the prompting of prayer. That I will be obedient when You call me to pray over my team. The season is long and will have its tough moments. God help me cling to Your strength and words for endurance and not cling to how the world says to go about it. Help lead me to be a light for my teammates in the dark moments. Speak truth into my heart so I can speak that same truth to my teammates. I love You, Lord. Amen!

Encouraging Words For My Team

_____

_____

_____

_____

_____

_____

_____

_____

_____

_____

_____

_____

_____

_____

_____

_____

_____

_____

_____

_____

_____

_____

_____

_____

Living Like Christ

[1 JOHN 2:6]

Whoever says he abides in him ought to walk in the same way in which he walked.

Living Like Christ

Dear God,

In a world filled with pride, selfishness, confusion, and doubt lead me in the way to walk just like Christ did. To be a light in this athletic community. Help me extend love and grace to those I don't feel deserve it because God the truth is I don't deserve it either. But because of Your grace, You have gifted it to me. Remind me that serving and loving my teammates first is the mindset I should have. Get rid of any pride or selfishness in my heart, for that is not of You, Lord. Prune me of anything that is not of You. Guide me in ways I can walk like Christ. I love You, Lord. Amen!

Living Like Christ

Being A Light In The Athletic Community

[JOHN 8:12]

When Jesus spoke again to the people, he said, "I am the light of the world. Whoever follows me will never walk in darkness, but will have the light of life.

Being A Light In The Athletic Community

Dear God,

You call us to be a light for Your Kingdom and God I want to shine that light in the athletic community. I am praying the bold prayer of wanting to be a vessel for You. I want to be an example of how to live a life that glorifies you, God. Fill my heart with Your truth and guide me in the way You see me as a vessel for your Kingdom. Give me the words to speak, guide me in my actions, and point out the teammates I can pray for. I want to be a prayer warrior for my teammates. I love your Kingdom and I want people to experience it. I love You, Lord. Amen!

Being A Light In The Athletic Community

Humility

[JAMES 4:6]

But he gives us more grace. That is why
Scripture says: "God opposes the proud but
shows favor to the humble.

Humility

Dear God,

Get rid of any pride I may be carrying in my heart and posture it to be a heart filled with humility. Knowing that pride is not of You in any way and walking in humility is how Jesus would act. Knowing that only fools think their way is right and never listen to anyone else. I crave to be more like Jesus. Convict me when I am walking out a life of pride and help me switch those words to words of gratitude. I am grateful for the sport I can play, my teammates whom I step on the court with, my coaches, and my athletic ability. Lead my heart to be in the posture of humility. I love You, God. Amen

Humility

Protection Against Injuries

[PSALM 46:1]

God is our refuge and strength, a very present
help in trouble.

Protection Against Injuries

Dear God,

I pray for the protection from injuries that I or my teammates could have this season. I want to thank You for a healthy body and one that can go through a lot of endurance during practice and games. I pray God for discernment when it comes to rest. To not overwork my body in an unhealthy way but understand that rest is very important when it comes to recovery. I pray over any athlete right now who finds themselves injured that they have a speedy recovery and encouragement during this time. Remember to steward even the seasons dealing with injuries well. I love you, Lord. Amen!

Protection Against Injuries

A Prayer For Gameday

[JOSHUA 1:9]

Have I not commanded you? Be strong and courageous. Do not be frightened, and do not be dismayed, for the Lord your God is with you wherever you go.

A Prayer For Gameday

Dear Lord,

I pray over my game today. I pray to play with excellence and steward my athletic ability well. I pray for safety as we travel to and from the game. Whether it is my team, the opponents, or the fans traveling to the game I pray to cover their drive. God, I pray that you lead my heart to serve and encourage my teammates. To remind them they are capable. Even when the game might not be going our way. I pray over my mindset that it is slow to anger and quick to encourage. I pray that I play for something bigger than myself. For You and my teammates. Thank You, God, for the ability to play the sport I love. I love You, God. Amen!

A Prayer For Gameday

A Prayer For Leadership

[JAMES 1:12]

Blessed is the one who perseveres under trial
because, having stood the test, that person
will receive the crown of life that the Lord has
promised to those who love him.

A Prayer For Leadership

Dear God,

I pray over my leadership. I pray that I embody the gifts you have given me. I pray that when I step into a leadership role whether that is for a play or the whole season I lead with love and humility. I ask You God to lead me to be the leader that Christ would be. I strive to live a life closely to how He did. Give me the right words to say during tough conversations, give me the heart to serve my team in the hard moments, and guide me in actions of love towards my team even when I feel like it's hard. I pray I speak with wisdom. I pray I speak words of life. Thank You for the gifts You have placed in my heart and help me steward them well. I love You, Lord. Amen!

A Prayer For Leadership

_____

_____

_____

_____

_____

_____

_____

_____

_____

_____

_____

_____

_____

_____

_____

_____

_____

_____

_____

_____

_____

_____

Courage Stepping On The Court

[1 CORINTHIANS 15:58]

Therefore, my dear brothers and sisters, stand firm. Let nothing move you. Always give yourselves fully to the work of the Lord, because you know that your labor in the Lord is not in vain.

Courage Stepping On The Court

Dear God,

I pray and ask You to give me the courage and strength to step onto the court. When times of doubt flood my mind Your strength takes over. There are times when the opponent seems to be unbeatable. But God I need You in those moments to find the courage to step into my ability as an athlete. To be reminded of the confidence I should carry because of the hours of preparation I have put into this game to compete. No matter if we win or lose, I need to play with excellence and not laziness. The lies of the enemy do not exist in my mind. The power of Your truth lives in my heart and my head. I love You, Lord. Amen

Courage Stepping On The Court

_____

_____

_____

_____

_____

_____

_____

_____

_____

_____

_____

_____

_____

_____

_____

_____

_____

_____

_____

_____

_____

_____

_____

Staying Calm During Adversity

[JAMES 1:2-4]

Count it all joy, my brothers, when you meet trials of various kinds, for you know that the testing of your faith produces steadfastness. And let steadfastness have its full effect, that you may be perfect and complete, lacking in nothing.

Staying Calm During Adversity

Dear God,

Guide me in a calm heart and headspace during times of adversity. God, I know you care so much about every little detail in my life. Whether that is an injury, a fight with a teammate, or a rocky relationship with a coach... God you care. Remind me that I can submit to You anything and You will fight for me. Let all my burdens be cast to You. Nothing can stand in your way and thank You for fighting my battles. I pray my heart leads with love during adversity and calls on you as my firm foundation. That when adversity strikes I act out of patience and godly wisdom. I love You, Lord. Amen!

Staying Calm During Adversity

Remembering God's Presence

[DEUTERONOMY 31:6]

Be strong and courageous. Do not fear or be in dread of them, for it is the Lord your God who goes with you. He will not leave or forsake You.

Remembering God's Presence

Dear Lord,

Thank You that Your presence is all around me. I don't have to pray for your presence I just need to acknowledge You are here. My heart is open for You to flood it. I want a heart God that welcomes you into every space I am in and every hard time I may face. In practice, a game, or a team dinner, Holy Spirit I invite You in. I acknowledge Your presence on the court with me. Your presence is powerful God and my source. Holy Spirit flow to me so that You can flow through me. I am here God. Thank You for being with me always. I love You, Lord. Amen!

Remembering God's Presence

To Remember God's Truth

[JOHN 14:6]

Jesus said to him, "I am the way, and the truth, and the life. No one comes to the Father except through me.

Dear Lord,

You know more than anyone that as an athlete I can be so hard on myself. I often find myself not speaking kindly when I mess up. God, I pray that You remind me to speak and think life-giving words over my life. Mistakes will happen but who I am is not compared to that mistake. I am sorry God for all the times I have spoken so poorly over Your creation. You made me in Your image and I never want to bash your creation. I pray that in moments of doubt about who I am, You remind me that I am chosen, I am able, and I am strong because of You. Thank You, God, for Your words of life. I love You, Amen!

To Remember God's Truth

God's Will For My Athletics

[JEREMIAH 29:11]

For I know the plans I have for you," declares the LORD, "plans to prosper you and not to harm you, plans to give you hope and a future.

God's Will For My Athletics

Dear Lord,

I submit to You the sport I love. I give You my athletic ability and want Your will over this journey in my life. God I pray that the sport I play never becomes an idol and if it does please convict me on the spot. Being an athlete is such a special gift You have given me and I want to be obedient to the plan You have for me. Use my athletic ability in a way that brings others to Your glorious kingdom. So that one day we can be playing one verse one with each other in Heaven. Your will be done over my athletic career, Lord. I love you. Amen!

God's Will For My Athletics

Amen!

Get Connected

www.coachjaetaft.com
Instagram.com/Coachjaetaft
Youtube.com/Coachjaetaft
Tiktok.com/coachjaetaft

See you there!

Made in United States
Troutdale, OR
03/09/2025